The Apprentice of Fever

Wick Poetry First Book Series
Maggie Anderson, Editor

Already the World
Victoria Redel   Gerald Stern, Judge

Likely
Lisa Coffman   Alicia Suskin Ostriker, Judge

Intended Place
Rosemary Willey   Yusef Komunyakaa, Judge

The Apprentice of Fever
Richard Tayson   Marilyn Hacker, Judge

The Apprentice of Fever

Poems by

Richard Tayson

The Kent State
University Press

Kent, Ohio, &

London, England

Library of Congress Catalog Card Number 96-12684
ISBN 0-87338-614-0 (cloth)
ISBN 0-87338-615-9 (pbk.)
Manufactured in the United States of America

05 04 03 02 01 00 99 98   5 4 3 2 1

The Wick First Book Series is sponsored by the Stan and Tom Wick Poetry Program and the
Department of English at Kent State University.

Library of Congress Cataloging-in-Publication Data

Tayson, Richard, 1962–
    Apprentice of fever : poems / by Richard Tayson.
        p.   cm.—(Wick poetry first book series)
    ISBN 0-87338-614-0 (alk. paper). —ISBN 0-87338-615-9 (pbk. : alk. paper)
    I. Title. II. Series.
    PS3570.A986A85 1998
    811'.54—dc21
                                                                    98-12684
                                                                    CIP

British Library Cataloging-in-Publication data are available.

CONTENTS

ACKNOWLEDGMENTS

My thanks to the editors of the following publications in which these poems first appeared, sometimes in earlier versions: "The Ice Cube" and "What Stops Me Sometimes Doctor," *Chelsea; "Sacraments"* and "Your Bath," *Crazyhorse;* "After *The Vanishing"* and "The Chase," *Global City Review;* "The Ascension," "My Mother Asks if Men Make Love Face to Face," and "Nightsweats," *Hanging Loose;* "The Gift," "Love as an Argument in Time and Loss," "Remembering the Man Who Molested Me," and "Sacred Anus," *The James White Review;* "Blood Test" and "Fever," *The Kenyon Review;* "In Sickness and in Health," *Michigan Quarterly Review;* "Prophylactic," *Minnesota Review;* "Peschanka," "Phone Sex," and "Your Feet," *The Paris Review;* and "First Sex," "James Dean as Eurydice," "Skin," "'Where Youth Grows Pale, and "Spectre-thin, and Dies,'" *Prairie Schooner.*

"Blood Test" and "Your Feet" were reprinted in *Jugular Defences: An AIDS Anthology* (1994), "First Sex," in *The Pushcart Prize XXI* (1996); "Blood Test," "In Sickness and in Health," "Peschanka," in *Things Shaped in Passing: More "Poets for Life" Writing from the AIDS Pandemic* (1997).

"James Dean as Eurydice," "Skin," "'Where Youth Grows Pale, and Spectre-thin, and Dies,'" and "First Sex" were awarded *Prairie Schooner*'s Bernice Slote Award and are reprinted by permission of the University of Nebraska Press.

My gratitude to Galway Kinnell, Dana Levin, Kenny Fries, Peter Meiland, Debra Kang-Dean, Cynthia Wakeley, Haas Mroue, and everyone at Kent State University who helped make this book possible, including Maggie Anderson, Alice Patterson, Will Underwood, Erin Holman, Diana Dickson, and Joanna Hildebrand Craig.

FOREWORD BY MARILYN HACKER

The Apprentice of Fever is a brilliantly corporeal first book, focused with lapidary clarity on the transfiguration of quotidian experience, its appetites, its unassuageable longings. From the start, the book's immediacy is rooted in the day-to-day life of a man implicated in the AIDS epidemic; living on the edge; crossing, transforming, and transgressing boundaries; always, always paying extreme and active attention, which is the apotheosis of compassion, which is an act of love. The narrator's lover has AIDS; his own status is moot; he is a young man who grew up, who assumed his sexuality in the shifting climate of the plague. Yet these poems are neither elegies nor protests. They are, in the main, love poems in which the focus, charged with desire and with memory, on the lover's body, is necessarily also a focus on mutability, on the body's other transformations, on the minutiae of illness, on the fevers, altered consciousness, self-abandonment, which sometimes cruelly resemble the *extasis* of sex, sex which is present in memory and in desire, which remains a creative force in the face of an illness for which it was, itself, the vehicle.

How much detail this poet notices! His close-ups are cinematic: a beloved face, a body, noted down to the razor nick on a chin, haircut-stubble at the nape, the wood-tick freckles on the shoulders and back—but also curly-leafed green bok choy on a kitchen counter, the life-blood of orange juice, a phallic cannoli. . . . And it is by this fine observation that the heights and depths of love (and rage) are communicated to the reader.

This would be enough, but it is not all. Tayson has also created formally complex longer sequences which synthesize the mythic and the erotic and raise them to Rilkean meditations. And he is, by his observer's nature, a poet of place, the place being Manhattan, its streets, *bodegas,* rooftops, fire escapes.

Every young poet at once invents her/himself and writes with a fugal counterpoint of influences. For Richard Tayson they are, perhaps, Cavafy, Adrienne Rich, Hart Crane, Sharon Olds; Ginsberg and Rukeyser in his celebrations of the body's "least speech." I also think of the young French writer, Hervé Guibert, brilliant urban outlaw and chronicler, entomologist of family interactions and betrayals, whose years living with AIDS were a core of magma for a scintillant talent. But Tayson's own voice is unmistakable: direct, witty, passionate, and desperate, in poems with the crucial acid to etch themselves on the reader's consciousness.

Marilyn Hacker

PART ONE

PHONE SEX

Sometimes I am so lonely the phone
will do.
Sometimes I am so lonely and you are not
dead, you
live in Brooklyn Heights yet I cannot
touch you.
I have spent thirty years trying not to write
this poem.
Sometimes I am so lonely the phone
will do.

.

Under the paper lantern of sleep, the sudden memory: living in Colorado,
pulling on my boots, going out into the blizzard, the snow burning a hole in
my tongue. I am nearly frozen, standing in front of a house unfamiliar to us
both, knowing you will take me in, and we will make angry love in front of
the fire. I let you take not gently the clothes from me. I would have done
anything you wanted: the prosthetic devices, the rope, the food, I made
myself sticky with honey and let you have this and that part of me, I was
stuck like paper to the wall, letting you have me dry, then wet, while your
wife looked on from her photo by the bed.

.

*You will be automatically matched with the next caller or will hear radio until
the next caller becomes available. To speak to somebody else press the pound key
under the 9 on your touch-tone dial.*

.

Black fishnet stockings
clothespins clamped to his nipples
bananas by the bed   bowl
of water   soap   green washcloth
razors   banana in his mouth   he slits
the skin with his teeth   razor
in my hand   his black hairs
come off the blade like scales:

summer, 1970. I am eight,
Kenny skins the fish
on the dock, throws the guts
in the lake, watches
the heavy blood sink. Skin
white as buttocks beneath the moon.

He bleeds slowly
never moans
arms and legs
splayed   kindergarten star
banana halfway in him   he arches
his back   two, then
three
then six
then myself

press the pound key to speak to
somebody else

eat white banana meat
iron-smell of blood

press the pound key to speak to
somebody else

he wants to tell me his fantasy.

•

In Puerto Rico your wife looks at me from across the table. Your two-year-old
daughter pees on the floor. The air sticky as pee. I look into your wife's eyes
then over at you by the window, your back to us. Your son bounces a red ball
into the apartment, sings in Spanish. He called me "Papi Dos" today, put your
hand in mine as we walked through the town. That was the moment I trace
back to my self-hatred. Your wife looks at me. Sticky sweet of overripe
mangoes on the table. She has left Argentina for this. You have told her the
truth, or the nearest approximation: *Faeries de Norteamérica, Pájaros de la*
Habana, Jotos de Méjico, Sarasas de Cádiz, Apios de Sevilla, Cancos de Madrid,
Floras de Alicante, Adelaidas de Portugal. And your wife stares at me from
across the table.

99 cents per minute, maximum of twenty minutes

I want you to talk dirty to me

Beat your cock against the receiver

in a glass elevator in a park on a see-saw against a tree
on the edge of a bridge on the hood of my father's car

press the pound key

tied up, my mouth gagged

Slap it around a little bit

or you will hear radio until the next caller

Finger it

anyone over fifteen is not my style

Slap it around a little bit

under the 9 on your touch-tone dial

I love all men's cocks

Finger it

Slap it.

•

I have spent thirty years trying not to write
this poem.

    Who fucked you, how many times, and where?

I knew you were there before I heard your voice
yelling *Bravo!* when the bassoonist finished her concert.
Trying not to look at me.
Your red corduroy shirt flashing
as you left the music hall.
Colorado night, sweet clear summer, sweet clear soul,
we're talking again, outside the music hall.
Nightfall.
Your hand grips my hand.
Soap bubbles in the tub, you want to sleep with me.
Even after I say no you crawl through the window.

      Who fucked you, how many times?

You knew I would fall in love that night.

          •

*I was ready to finish your letter last night but as usual something happened and
I couldn't. At work, started with vomits, my boss went to the pharmacy and
bought some medicines.*

      How many times and where?

*I haven't been feeling well, a lot of stomach ache, and I have some purple spots
on my chest.*

I have spent thirty years trying not to write
this poem.

          •

*Don't call every night, you're not rich, save your money to come
to San Juan.*

You said you had a magic phone.
It made free calls.
Don't waste your money, you said.
Call me late, I said.
Call me early, I said.
What about your wife? I said.

Every night
I felt your terror
though we had no name for
it.
Purple spots on your legs, arms, belly.
We had no name for
it.

Vomiting, don't call.

And when I called
you had a new boyfriend.
Golden boy, body builder, accountant.
Living in Brooklyn, you said.
I have my green card, you said.
We bought a king-size bed, you said.
We use the same toothbrush, you said.

Static on the line, the garbled buzz
of jammed signals. I hold out
for the right words
but get the fourth blond 6'2" blue-eyed
muscley twenty-three-year-old tonight
named David.

Under the gummed eyelid of sleep,
the tops and bottoms
become interchangeable, the sounds
melt down to slogans, acronyms, holy
ellipses

until words stick in my throat,
dissolve slowly,
with lessening pleasure
like the gum drops
Father brought home
then stopped bringing

home. Word:
something to lick, paw,
insert yourself into.
The need to name in a time
of silence.
I do not know if sex is an illusion,
says the woman to her lover
across the table. And I row

downriver toward limitless
sleep, float
on a wordless sea
in a bed-shaped raft.
Splinters in my palm
as I stitch your real name
to my crotch for the time
when you will be unable
to speak and I unable
to forget.

PART TWO

FEVER

All morning I look at the upside-down
fire escape veering into our apartment,
the metal steps ascending
to hell as you take the thermometer
from my mouth, tell me I have the flu,
then go out for the orange juice
I crave. The phone
rings, Tyler's voice tells me a woman
reversed her diagnosis,
her T-cell count climbing
and climbing until it went off
the scale. *Belief*
in the universal energy
is what did it, he says,
the woman became young again.
I tell him I don't believe
in white light or luck,
any age is as bad
as any other, the stink
sweating out of me, my tongue
rubbery as a cow's guttural
pink. Tyler says,
you'll never change, will you?
and goes on about self-
acceptance, loving
what we hate about ourselves.
I remind him of Andrew's
pneumocystis carinii, Larry's
black lesions, Brian's
mycobacterium avium,
the rifabutin Roberto is testing, Vito's
death. I think of my
hair falling into the sink, my father
puking on the bathroom
floor, my mother
riding off on the next-door neighbor's
motorcycle and I
hang up as you come through
the door with the grocery sack

of magic. You pull out one thing
after another: the chicken
soup lays a fuchsia egg from its
tin bottom, the naked
man on the cover of *Blueboy* is now
the woman who climbs into the coffin-
shaped box to be severed in half
then made whole again. The jar
glistens with orange blood
cells as you show me
the blue boy's healthy
organs opening page after page
as if to mock us, you lift
the juice to my lips, your eyes
glowing bright as new planets above me.

BLOOD TEST

As the needle goes into my arm
I think of the moment
we first got into bed together:
your body prone along mine,
your shaved head against
my ribs. I kiss the stubble,
think how your anger
is the only thing you have left
as your body fails, blood cell
by blood cell. The nurse
fingers my pulse, asks
if I have nightsweats, any
unhealed marks on my body
and when I say *no,* I
hear your question as you
reach for the extra-strong
condoms on the table. You
hover over me, I
feel your swelling
between my thighs, you could
tear my inner membranes, expose
my blood to your own
and when I say no, you
want me to say it
again and again, your eyes
closing as you fling your
seed across my body until
I hear the nurse say she's
going to take the needle
out of my arm, straight
out of me. She's
quick to place the round
of cotton over the opening
and I think of the coin
placed over the eyes of
the dead. I
see the white drops of your
sperm on my stomach, watch
as your eyes open and

you see that I want it
off my body. You wet
your fingertips with the glutinous
fluid, shake them in my
face, saying *this is it, man,*
the only life we have now.

I didn't know what the movie was about
but I was angry at you for not wanting
health insurance or western
medicine, I phoned 777-FILM
and found the closest theater with a 2:45,
I put on my winter coat and said
"it's your life, not mine, I'm going to a show."
I didn't know it would be about losing
the person you love in the prime
of your life together, I stood
on the corner of Henry and Orange
and heard the voice of Louise Hay,
her meditations you kept playing
over and over until I hoped
she'd become mute in some tragic accident,
I sat down in the dark to forget you.
And then the lovers were in love,
they drove into a tunnel
and ran out of gas,
they argued and she walked
into the fog and he walked
into the sun, and she thought
about dying alone, without anyone
to rock her safely in the cradle
of his arms, he drove
out of the tunnel and found her.
He didn't know that the first loss
was preparation for the big one,
the one you sometimes see in the movies
where the evil person looks sweet,
a man with a broken arm
selling key rings, someone
you could see in a convenience store
and speak with, as she does, leaning
against his car while he shows her
the key ring with her boyfriend's initials
engraved on the front. She gets in
and feels the seat plush as a mother's
breast, he takes the poisoned handkerchief

and covers her mouth, as if with one
deep kiss, at the exact right moment,
and she faints, the way I fainted
the day the doctors told us
you were going to die. Not today
or tomorrow, but soon, and the camera
goes underground, the leading woman
wakes and is not in her lover's arms
or in her own bed, the earth
packed around her tight as her lover's
lips sealing her lips,
she screams, beats her fists
against the coffin's lid, and I don't
wait for the final credits but run
home and open the door, saying
your name over and over, bathroom
to bedroom, and you're there, naked
in bed, silent, not dead, wanting
me to touch you, palm, back,
nipple, mouth, we make love
in the uncaged air.

THE ICE CUBE

On the hottest night of the summer,
we drink mango juice,
and you tell me your nightmare:
you have jungle fever, you say,
you get in the plane
with your sixteen handsome escorts
and head for the tropics,
when the phone rings,
you're sunning yourself
in paradise, two natives
massaging your thighs.
You turn away when you tell me this,
sweat rolls down your temples,
and I tilt the Burger King cup
to my lips, swallow the juice
until there's only an ice cube left.
I take it in my mouth, reach over
and you think I'm going to whisper
how much I love suntans
and twenty dark fingers
kneading my muscles,
but I kiss you and slip
the ice into your mouth.
I feel it against your tongue
and think you're going
to swallow, but you give it back,
roll it against my palate,
I feel its drip inside me.
This is like passing words
back and forth, but silent, the solid
object has one meaning only.
But then I think it's hard as a coconut
skull, brittle
as toffee, smooth
as cut glass, our mouths
wet as the head of your—
but I don't want to say it,
I'm quick to take it
from your mouth and rub it

across your clammy chest, down
to the pucker of your belly button,
I do not want this to end.
But it diminishes, as time
diminishes, we pass it back and forth
more quickly now. You look at me
with the excitement of a man
who wants to feel pleasure
all night, your jaw
vibrates, like a bed creaking
beneath two bodies,
small crunching sound
as you drink our pleasure down.

NEW FOOD

One day we wake and you don't
go for the red meat but flush
the dark coffee grains down
the toilet, boil water for your yannoh.
I get out of bed, watch you
chuck eggs from the window, spill
milk over the sill, toss
tonight's spareribs down the laundry
chute and the steam of your yannoh
rises. You cram king-size
garbage bags with cheeze
spread, Hungry Man
TV dinners, go for the box
of cannolis, your mouth
frothy and rabid as when you
used to take the candied apple
of my sex in your hand. I say
I'll fight to the death for those,
you say, *eat 'em now cuz when I get*
back they're gone for good and drag
the food out the door. I sit beside
the pile of soap bars and Barbasol
cans and disposable shavers, open
the box, take the long
chocolate in my hand, thrust
my tongue into the hollow
where the wafer folds over
like skin, I take the rich cream
in my mouth, swallow
and swallow, I can't get
enough. By the time you come
home, I've had them all,
I say, *where's the god-*
damned coffee, you pull out
collard greens, lay baby
bok choy on the counter like a green
row of male paper dolls beside
the extra-firm tofu, turn on
the heat, slice daikon and shitake

mushrooms, you say you're going
to save your life. I say
be real—you float
the black hijiki in water,
put the miso and umeboshi
plums in the fridge, go on
about yoga, TM, scream and touch
therapy, turn, and I open
my legs, show you
the soft thistle-down of my cock.
You turn away, splash wet
tofu in the pan and I go
into the bathroom, face
the mirror wanting to beat myself
to a frenzy, the pain
so universal that I look like a man
who has come through history,
who knows the beginning of time,
a man who knows the end.

SKIN

When you come out of the bathroom
I see the blood where you
cut your throat, shaving. I say,
you should go easier on yourself.
You wipe the blood with a white cloth,
I see how thin you've become.
My palm brushes the swollen glands
in the crease above your thigh,
moves up your chest to where
you nicked the skin—I want to
taste it. I reach
up, touch your stomach, the red
smear glistens, touch
your thigh and the red
shines. I wonder why
you turn the blade against
yourself and I
see the scar on my wrist,
remember the day you spilled
boiling water and my skin
tore, revealing the white
membrane beneath. I move
my finger to my mouth, am filled
with rage and desire,
the tip of your cock milky
and swollen, you want me to do it.
But I don't do it:
I look out the window, understand
that the body is what we can
no longer give each other,
the danger we so easily could share.

I want to tell her I remember
how Father would close
their bedroom door, click
the brass lock quietly,
and how they made love without
a squeak, up on their lonely
hill, the white bedspread
patterned in lily-of-the-valley,
their bodies carefully corseted
in nipple-flesh
and button-
holes, my superhuman
parents gouged into one another.
When they looked down
they saw fruit on the earth,
climbed back to the postman,
an endless line of secretaries,
taught their children the art
of silence. I tell her
none of this and you come
into the room, a towel
around your waist, smelling
of shaving cream. I mouth *Mother,*
you turn to the mirror,
take the towel from your hips.
My mother talks about the acid
Jeffrey Dahmer used to dissolve
human bones, and I remember
the time I awoke with your body
behind me, how I felt
consciousness and lubrication
take me together, the woman in me
lodged deep in my urethra,
washed in waste until I turned
to you and said *no.* I wanted her
to live, felt her grin
inside me, crush

my left testicle between her teeth
as your eyes grew larger
and you moved inside my elastic
membrane, the nozzle
corkscrewing, the man in me
loving it, the pinioned wheel
turning and me in control,
the woman in me frothy with power,
muscular as my dreams.
You rub the antibacterial
cream on your razor cut,
the hydrocortisone gel
on the flaking red streaks above
your eyebrows, and I tell my
mother our bodies are ethereal,
we slip out of consciousness
and into the atmosphere, nothing
to cling to in space
but each other, your blue
eyeball close to my brown
eyeball, our two bodies
clamped into each other,
the sweat on your forehead
falling into my mouth, I take it
like wine from the chalice,
taste the chemical in your salt,
feel my blood flow free with it
as we lie in the world, just like the others.

FIRST ANNIVERSARY

On our first anniversary, after
we'd drunk one bottle of champagne,
we climbed to the roof. Rung
by rung, twelve
stories up, the second bottle
in the hip pocket of your fatigues,
you pulled me up the last hot
rung, as if helping me climb out
of the black pit inside myself.
You popped the cork, tipped
the foam into my mouth, not too dry,
not too sweet, just as your mouth
was not too dry the first time
we kissed, you took a long
swig, leaned close to my face
and I started to fall. Cliff edge,
corner stone, brick, I felt
your breath on my mouth
and knew you were not going
to die tonight or tomorrow, the rich
blood flowing in you still,
I suddenly bit your lip. June,
July, another life, I tasted
a drop of your blood
and went to the edge. The mystery
is not this city, or how it is one person
can know and not know another,
it is not how long we'll last
on this earth, the wind like God's
breath claiming us, I did not feel afraid.
I teetered and you called me back
to your arms, and I smelled
the rich odor of your body, the sweat
I could drink like rain
falling over us, button, zipper, nipple
ring, we left our bodies
behind. And when we came too close
to the sun, I felt myself fall

back into my body. I looked
closely in your eyes, Central
Park, Fifth Avenue, the maze
of the city inside you, standing on the ledge.

YOUR FEET

When we climbed the black stone,
I was already in love
with your feet. I hadn't
seen them up close, so
when we made it to the top
and you lifted them into my lap,
I was shocked at how small they were.
I rubbed my palm along the arch
and thought of the Chinese girl
whose mother broke her bones
and bound her feet in the rough
sackcloth, I pulled
your socks off and pressed
the rounded bone at the ball
of your sole, you moaned
that must be where my liver is,
toe joints I cracked,
that must be where your spine is.
So I held your spine and massaged
your brain—and that night
we molded our bodies together
for the first time, we kissed
for five years, twenty-three days
until the first purple spot
appeared on your foot.
You cried, I
cradled it, held it
to my mouth and sucked
the death cells out, I kissed
the lesion away, arch bone,
ankle joint, fibula, I learned
to love small things,
your mouth, fist
of earth, first snow, for better
and for worse, we
settled in for the duration.

PESCHANKA

(The Russian town near what is now Volgograd, where the German Sixth Army lost the battle of Stalingrad in the winter of 1943, and 250,000 soldiers died.)

I read about the man who stood
fifty years after the battle and saw
the field of human skeletons.
He bent close to the loamy earth
and took the photograph of one
skull, scream of the open
mouth, jawbone
broken, left molar
missing, and when I look up,
you sleep beside the open window.
You are letting the sun in, spring
in, your mouth open
against the ocher grain of the easy
chair, and suddenly you are not
breathing. I
put the magazine down, go to you,
touch your knee, when you do not
wake, I reach up, press
my hand to your mouth, as one who
wants to save another the torture
of slow death will place the pillow
over his face and press down
gently. I want to be
merciful, as I was told God is
merciful, I want to say, *lie down*
my love in the green pasture,
and then I feel the gold silk
of your breath on my palm,
and in my joy I close
the window, as if finally
locking the heavy cathedral
door. I touch
your shaved head, the stubble
pliant as grass shoots pressing
up through your skull, I pull

your mouth to mine,
and you breathe, it's
summer, the fever
takes you and beats you, as the man
in the photograph was taken and
beaten and left to die.

SACRED ANUS

You are putting your finger on the place
        never spoken,
I am remembering the baby in his crib,
        I am the baby
seeing the face of my motherfather, hearing
        the voice say
nice boys don't touch, your finger at my most
        private place.

I am letting your finger dip in and dip out,
        I am feeling
your breath on my thigh, then I am my thigh
        with your left hand holding,
I am your left hand, your finger, I am my anus
        opening and closing
around your finger, sea shell with the salt sea
        sifting in.

I am living in a place of air and blinds flapping,
        where men are not hurting
each other, I am feeling your first and second
        fingers slip in,
your thumb on the seam connecting my anus
        to my scrotum,
I am trying to say what even our rich language
        has no word for.

I am feeling your tongue along the place
        people call a crack,
though it's not a crack but a half-moon touching
        a half-moon, I am
the moon floating in thick placenta sky, you are
        slipping in and out
of me, the way high tide moves across the beach
        then retreats.

I am remembering Walt Whitman's twenty-eight
    young men whose bellies
swell to the sun, I am the twenty-eight young men
    lying on their backs,
you are the fifty-six hands exploring, three fingers
    then the cock
that is not fucking me but is the music
    my body's a string for.

PROPHYLACTIC

You tear the cellophane,
look down at me, pour
lubricant into your
palm, touch
yourself, and the slick
grease drips into
the crease of my thigh.
The white shape hovers
between us, insular
as a body inside an oxygen
tent, you turn, the cut
on your lip opens. The blood
swells gently out, the way
the tide swells onto the land
and I want out of bed:
I leave my body, drift
up along the wall, out
the window, watch
you peel back my flesh,
throw my legs over
your shoulders, lean
forward, lever
down, you work your hook
inside me. I think how
awkward we look doing this,
drift to other apartment
windows, see a couple
in each room doing the same
thing. I am the calm
witness of this ritual,
this trust in a millimeter
of latex: I fall
back inside myself, look
down at the kid-glove rubber
tearing the thin wall
of tissue, look up
as your eyes
close, your milk
fills the sack with those
thousand seeds of death.

NIGHTSWEATS

When I hear the guttural throatcall,
I tie the line around you, pull it
so you float toward me
like an unconscious swimmer.
I feel the wetness on my arm,
and think you are pissing or I am
sixteen and sleepwalking with a hard-on,
waking in time to see the arc
sluicing against Mother's new rug.
But I am twenty-eight and think you are
peeing on me, I turn to let it
douse my back but feel
the sheets wet and wake
fully and see
the sweat forcing its way
out, your whole skin
coming apart. You shudder
as if your bones have loosened,
I shake you, but you don't want to
leave the underwater lair of sleep,
I pull the blankets
down, remember
how I had lain before sleep
in the hollow bowl of your pelvis
and ribcage, cradled in the black
slime of pubic hairs, deep-sea flora
floating, how we fell asleep like that.
Now the horror in the dark
is the leak, the sweat
greasing your whole
torso, you don't wake
and I turn on the light,
shout, *wake up, it's a bad*
dream, you cry,
it hurts I'm scared, and I go
fill the tub because I don't know
what else to do, begging you
to climb into the cool water
before you catch fire, the whole ocean

a burning oil slick, the sweat
spilling on me
like gasoline, hot
wax, the sun
coming up as you climb in
to your chin, I keep
lifting your mouth above water,
crying as you sleep.

YOUR BATH

I open the door and see you
in the green water, the freckles
along your shoulders like wood
ticks, saw-toothed
snouts just above the river
of your blood, you begin scrubbing
your back. It's not easy
watching you do this, it takes
all your strength to lean
forward and clutch
the brush, shift
back and lather
the bristles, lift
your arm until I think
you are a man whose skin will
split as he leaves this world.
I will be calm, I go to the tub
and say, *here, let me do it for you,*
I am so young, so goddamned
healthy, I don't know how
to live with such guilt.
You turn and I peel
a tick from your shoulder, place it
between my lips and move
in the fog toward you, I will
eat a whole forest to spare you
this. You flinch and I see
how the pain has
beaten you, whipped you,
one lash for each of your forty-one
years, you say, *no, I'll do it
myself.* You push
your hands into the water, scoop
it over your head, silver
hairs, underarm
hairs, plough, burial, soap
stone, you cannot walk. I do not know
how to live with such guilt,
so I go to the living room,

turn on the TV, hear you toss
the death head on the floor,
pull the plug so the water
goes down the drain, taking
you with it, elbow, haunch,
hips, hand, ossified
feet whose bones God
eats over a flame blue
as health in the country
of the dead, I
run in and hear the gnashing
as you hit rock
bottom, God
spits you out and you land,
bruised and beaten,
in my faithless arms.

For a week you lie beneath one sheet,
the fever comes, your face
darkens, the way a boy's face will
flush, the forehead hairs
dampen when his father comes at him
with a fire prod. Then the chill
comes, you sleep
beneath five blankets, your body
shaking, as a boy will freeze
and crack along a fracture line
when his parents lock him out
on the coldest night of the year.
Your head rests heavily on the pillow,
your face pale then bright
with the pink blooms like bruises,
and I know you were a boy whose father
struck him with whatever was handy—
a rifle butt, a baseball bat,
a brick, once—
and I lift the blankets
as if parting the veil that separates
us from the next world. I touch
your underwear, checking for wetness,
smell your urine on my fingers
sweet as the life still in you,
slide the cloth down
your skinny hips and skinny legs,
take the sponge from the bowl
and clean you off. I wipe
the sticky sweet from your penis,
see how shriveled and clammy the skin is,
how the tiny hairs are braided
together, curled
as if frozen beneath ice
and I come even closer, see the pink
flush of the head, the greenish
web of veins on your thighs,
the mole on your left testicle.
I think how many times

you have wanted me to explore
your body, in love, and I
dry you off, pull up
a fresh pair of underwear, climb
into bed beside you. I press
my clothed body against your ribs,
shoulders, your fine intelligent face
with the nose I've come to love
despite its imperfection,
I feel your eyelids move
beneath my fingers
as you wake for the first time
in two days, and I kiss
your forehead and dirty
silver hair, comb out
the knots, your whole life
opening in the room.

THIS KNOWING

When I look down at my lover's
penis—the fur stole
curling up toward the base,
the thick underside that leads
up to the two swivel
balls I've watched him un-
screw to slip the ring
from the slit—I see the pearly
drop of liquid. I stop
and stare, thinking somewhere
inside him he is producing
an X or a Y chromosome, and I can
tell by the rise
in the crease
of his left eye that he likes
when I do this, I hear him moan.
I've heard it so often
I can distinguish the modulations
in its tone, I cannot stop
wondering if I will one day
die from this. When I broke
into a sweat last Wednesday,
and he brought me soup, all night
I thought of that drop,
the creamy pewter glaze of it,
the taste my tongue knows
with a fierce knowing—slightly
metallic with a finish sweet as squeezed
peaches—I wonder how many other people
are thinking of death tonight. Not this
summer, not this
man I would walk through fire for,
not this particular jism that
comes, slowly, at first,
then with such force it sometimes
shocks me, I do not know how
to love him. O yes I know
how to love him, the mouth
whose memory of our first

kiss is still in its quiet
cave, I cannot tell you
why I love this man. I cannot say why
we are on this earth, in every
city, township, *arrondisement,*
I cannot talk about this mystery
in any terms but the physical. Then the higher
note comes, the one that sometimes
turns into a yell, the sweat
falls from my forehead
onto his chest, and his mouth
closes as the liquid shower comes
and the white juice shines like glutinous
rain God flings down from his
house, holy, substantial, flesh
of the one who takes you there,
singing, this marriage.

PART THREE

In the photograph
the dying man begins
the spin
back
in time, toward the moment
he will be
weightless, his bones
porous as pumice stone.
His fingers
are nubs, frail,
weblike. His father's
hands
curve round the crown
of his head,
touch the ear that cannot
hear
anything
but the buzz of flies,
growing louder.
The father
touches his son's
cheek, the bone
pronounced as
stone,
ready to break,
to spill forth the inner
fibrous dust
of the world.
There in the room
the father is weeping.
The painting of superhuman hands
wants to lift
that body
into—what? The father
touches his head
to his son's
mass of dead brain
cells, wipes away

the gummy inner mucus
from his son's
lips. The dying
young man feels—what?
Perhaps a gratefulness
I have never known,
the ease of death giving
his face a brightness
I saw in Masaccio's
Holy Trinity. Even
the light in the painting
behind the father's
head
touched to his son's
head
is the light of
heaven.
The living are assuaged.
I look up into—what?
There is the mirror
where each morning
I stand marveling
the miracle of skin
and bone, the fact
of the light, the myths.

JAMES DEAN AS EURYDICE

1

When I met _____ I dreamed of coming up from underneath
the earth without seeing his face turning until we were all the way

out into the beginning into the white burning.
I dreamed of coming up as a star

Natalie Wood crying into my leather jacket
and me the kid trying to save her. But that was before

I went underneath, before I met _____
and drank with him all night
first at the Silverlake Runaround
where I stayed in the back in the dark
away from the schoolgirls trying to throw me

up into the light into the burning. Later at _____'s estate
me not used to mixing drinks, _____
rubbing ice across my lips the hollow of my throat
hollow tinkling of glass music stirring the metal prong

my fingers burning in the dark in the heat
_____ reaching over with the gin
our hands touching, corporate America watching
as I went down so cold so statue I swear I was a god.

2

_____was checking off names as I came into the room.
He walked to where I was sitting in a corner memorizing
lines, put his hand over my elbow, held it, his palm pressing

pressing to go beneath my skin. Later I took the glass
from him, my fingers feeling

down down the black
passageway down step by step into
the silence the awkward
clothes sticking everywhere to my skin, down

45

down. I went way under one night in sleep
my breath like the drink just finished.

I went dancing along the stones by the river
lost in the darkness forever, hearing his strange

melodies, looking for the claims of his lyre. I found
bourbon on a silver tray beneath the willow
as I drank it got darker I knew
I would never find him I was underneath
looking up waiting for his shadow to descend singing
acting the way he'd taught me
the way I'd seen the pros do it. I took his absence

like I took my face in the river watching
heard the song up and down the barbed wire staff
knowing the god in me was dead.

4

I sat on the rocks waited for _____ to speed my going
or stop it, needed another drink something
to insert myself into somewhere to lose my body
to resurrect the god in me. Then the miracle

better than Hollywood:
I couldn't see his face anymore I was lost
in the shade, no conjuring his shape. When I couldn't
see his eyes over the shot glass
his face above the paper as he ticked
pencil marks, when
I couldn't smell the bourbon of his breath as his face
hovered over my dying coming closer I knew
what freedom was what joy was no one knew me.
I licked my lips felt the redundancy
of clothes threw my jacket

into the river with the barge passing all night over
watched the skin
sinking I forgot the face
looming over my own forgot the tongue of _____

heard the silence of dark the rustle of my body
as it got up and left the scene
walked out into the dark fig and narcissus forgot
even his name. Then

5

I heard the singing down the shaft
of light of gray of personality I saw
his hands tearing the darkness to pieces the eyes
I remembered up close. I felt his tongue going down
over me like the cadence of song, that throbbing
song I wished him dead I wanted
to be left forever in the shade
feeling my body as another form of dark. Now he

presses me to go back up into the light
into the cluttered world tempts me forever
up the long shaft I never thought
I'd be the one to follow up into the consuming
the god chasing the human.

FIRST SEX

When we found your father's *Playboys*,
we went into your room and touched
the glossy tanned breasts of the naked
woman on the beach, you pressed
her unblemished skin against the milk-
white flesh of your twelve-year-old
body, I kissed my virginal
lips to your lips and your father
walked in. I don't remember, now,
who had his pants down or who was
lying like a seed in the center
of the photos leafed around him,
all I remember is your father
stood in the doorway, shapely
as God, bearded, big-stomached, right
fist clenched, he wanted to eat us.
Yes, I tell you, fathers eat their sons.
I closed my eyes and waited for him
to tear away my best friend's leg
or carve a rib-bone from his
untouched chest, I heard
the voice of my father:
Are you a girl? Do you know what evil
is? Are you a girl?
Are you? But my body proved I was
not a girl, if God
was about to send the flood
waters up over us, I must be
Satan, the spermatozoa hatching
like polliwogs in the twin fishbowls
of my testicles, and the kiss
I wanted even then, the work of Satan.
Your father began yelling in his deep
male voice, the earth
shook, I
opened my eyes and thought he would
hit us with the bed or
bury us beneath a wall or two,
but he gave us one final

look and slammed the door
behind him: we were forever
separate from God, father, son, holy
spirit, we faced each other
in the dark and entered manhood.

THE CHASE

I don't remember where he was taking us
but the radio was on,
Father tapped his wedding ring
against the steering wheel
and whistled like he always did
when he was away from my mother.
Maybe we were going to get a fifth
of something or other,
up Telephone Road, I wasn't fighting
with my brother, I was lulled
by the even keel of the engine, the car
so full of sun you would have thought
life was bliss, narcotic, I was
numb when the red sports car
pulled in front of us. Father hit
the brakes, my seat belt
tightened, as if someone had reached
his hands up through the chassis
and was pulling me by the waist,
but my body lurched out of his grip
and we stopped before we smashed
into that car. The couple inside
didn't know they'd pulled in front
of us, they were drugged by the smell
of the ocean on a clear day,
I think they even kissed, and Father
pounded his fist against the horn
and said, *goddamn guy's drivin' worse
than a woman.* I looked
at my brother, and the Porsche
pulled away, but Father couldn't
stand it, he leaned out his window
and yelled, *whose ol' lady taught you
to drive,* and the guy
heard, his arm appeared, he flipped
my father the finger and that was it,
Father gunned it
and the guy saw us coming so he
gunned it, we flew

up the on ramp to Highway 101 doing
sixty, the Porsche darted easily
in and out of traffic, we were
losing him but I was proud
to be on the racetrack
with such a competent driver.
I remembered Father saying
when you hit a guy
you have to lean your weight into it,
so he floored it, we almost hit
a school bus, Father smiled
as if anger made him happy, his eyes
lit up bright as radar in the pupils
of the Six Million Dollar Man, I was
staring at a hole in the seat cover
where Mother's shoulder usually was
when my brother spotted the Porsche
turning into the J. C. Penney Center
where Mother liked to shop.
Father cut off two cars
and made a quick right, I thought
he would fly through the plate
glass store front or smash
that car to pieces, but he slammed
the station wagon into park
and jumped out like Clark Kent
bounding up through the phone booth
to show his two young boys how
to treat people in public, he grabbed
the driver's door and raised
his fist and reached in
to pull the guy out, when his face
turned blood red, his mouth
slackened, his body
went limp, as if he'd never seen
a woman before.

REMEMBERING THE MAN WHO MOLESTED ME

His mouth opens and closes like a hinged
shell, his tongue studded with red
barnacles, the way river stone is
encrusted with tiny mollusk shells,
sucking protein. I smell
whiskey, his eyes hover toward
me, the way spotlights float under
water, his hands
huge as black flippers. His blood
beats against his wrist pressed
to my belly as he goes for
my nipple, his hands
like great webbed feet of an animal
rising from the pond's dark
bottom. He chews my
nipple like seaweed, gnawed rubber,
and I rise above the water, am suddenly
the omnipotent god watching over all
the children. Before his fingernails tear
my inner membranes, before
he grabs my hair and yanks
my head and shoves
his swollen purple-veined penis
head to the back of my throat
and I gag on the sperm of my father's best
friend, I take over: I fill
my mouth with fish
hooks, loop fishing line
around my neck, stuff
lead sinkers into my ass, cover
my head and hairless sex with yellow
pond flowers, I sink
down past the protean
insects and gold
fish, down
to the pond's bottom—I save myself, drift
down, feel my skin compose with fish
bone and bacteria, the black
silt and polliwogs' bellies, I say,
you may now have this child.

WHAT STOPS ME SOMETIMES DOCTOR

What stops me sometimes Doctor
is a puff
a toke
an open me up and take me
down and dirty now   stone
in my blood. What stops me

is one of my four
voices   the one with that
beautiful-by-ugly-by-beautiful
face attached   my mother
what stops me

is her seven-'til-thirteen-year-old
thighs spread
open by her stepfather's
hands   the way he'd
skin the lid off a can of peanuts

and sometimes Doctor a man's fingers
in my mouth is her mouth
is what happened next
and why not   my mouth
lived safely in her body nine months
is what happened next
and made her eat two pounds of chocolate
every afternoon   made her

silent all my life
made her want to be ugly so no one would
look at her   and what makes me

want seed
want no tree
want speed
want no car
want smoke
want no sky

want sight
want no eyes
want you

to put it in   put it
in I say   stay out   put it
in   don't speak   it's our

secret   Mother we can't
go forward because of the light
he swallowed from your split
womb   so now the
light up take these snort this have a sip buy you a drink kid
doesn't that make you feel a whole lot better?

thing that goes through me in that fatherly
voice says   Doctor
from the inside out
I'm nothing but
junk.

THE GIFT

I do not like to remember
the three of us driving north
on 101 at sunset, the sand below
like a margin of broken glass.
I do not like to remember
the gold sheen of my cousin's
mustache, as he turned his head,
for just a second,
to look back at me.
And I do not like to remember
that I liked the big hands
and the black hair of the man
beside him, the deep male timbre
of their voices as they talked,
as it darkened. We were going seventy
past the eucalyptus groves
of Carpenteria, Terry looked
away from the road, and then
it happened—he held Bill's
hand, caressing each knuckle,
he ran his finger along the lifeline
stretching like a road before him,
and suddenly my life became clear to me.
I felt the car edge toward the sea,
Terry kept looking at Bill,
I could not take my eyes from them,
I could not speak, I don't know how
to say this, I saw the sheer
drop of the cliff, the white
caps, the waves, I saw
my father's face, five feet under,
and deeper down the face
of the Christian god, bobbing up
in his wet suit. Then the car
spun out of control, forced
its way through the guard-
rail, like a penis tearing a virgin
man's anus, and I smelled eucalyptus
burning stronger than the odor

of my kin's flesh burning, we were
trapped inside a flaming
metal carcass, for just a second,
those two hands soldered together
at the wrists, still
holding each other, fingers
fixed in place in my universe,
and then the car stopped.
I do not like to remember
Terry hopping onto the beach,
opening Bill's door and pulling
him out, they were
laughing and kissing and taking
off their clothes and kissing,
a dam in me was breaking,
the flood waters rushing
over my body, the dead
crayfish calling *Goddamn, Goddamn,*
like black birds high above
the earth, underwater, and I swam up,
naked, looked at the two of them
walking toward the moon, calling out
my name, each with his gift
held out so lovingly to the other.

[Patroclus and Achilles]

Was it the way Patroclus touched anger to his skin
    in the form of armor
and retreated from love that made them both think
    of endings? Was it
the tent flaps closing, the ache of silence after,
    that made Achilles see
the time before: Patroclus tossing grain to the goats,
    letting the small black heads

huddle against his hands, was it the image throbbing
    in the head wound of silence
that made the past blur the present argument? Achilles
    remained alone,
the heat pressing against the tent walls, Patroclus's voice
    rising in his mind,
the distant sound of war making him see again the green
    scrim of cypress surrounding

the past, letting them have the world on their own terms.
    Was it the face
of Patroclus held in place by Achilles's hands pressing,
    that made love
the ache for the present tense and allowed the grass
    to be another form
of skin, Achilles's hands touching sand, grass, black hair
    in one gesture, undoing

the leather ties, as if the removal of clothing was longing
    for a future.
He hears the argument in his mind, the battle beyond
    the tent, the sea
the day he hung clothes over the branches, nothing
    stopping the lovers
from feeding each particular desire, pressing down
    the earth with their flesh,

releasing, pushing forward into the unknowable, the quick
     breathing in the lemon-hung
air, their bodies taken into the sound of the sea sucking
     the earth below.
Was it the gradual failure of light that made Achilles see
     the body beneath him
differently, the face upturned with a sorrowful joy
     only the loved know,

Patroclus's hands feeling the dome of Achilles's forehead,
     leading his tongue
there, yes, along the place of vulnerability, his hands
     holding time still,
the armored body advancing into another form of argument,
     the sun
striking the metal protection with bright stars of wounds,
     the body

insisting on another identity, the lover and the loved
     finally one, the lie
removed like a mask as the eyes bleed from their sockets
     like wine from the mouth
of the lover into the mouth of the loved, the sky
     bleeding into cypress,
was it the ache of the past that made Achilles run out
     into the bloodletting?

Suddenly, at the climax of making
love, I leaned close
to your face, my legs draped
like wings over your thighs,
and you found the place in my back
where the heat comes out of me,
just between the wings
of my shoulder blades, real entry
to my soul. I saw that knowing
look in the center of your eyes
where the blue becomes white,
you didn't touch the place
of my willing powerlessness,
you held your hand above it,
the wings sprouted on either side of it,
breaking open, gently. You stopped
moving inside me, you lay
very still inside me, and suddenly
I was afraid. You saw my fear
and kissed me, not a deep
tongue kiss, but a light
touch of your tongue on my teeth,
and then we started to rise
together, up and across
a border, our spirits
flying out the tops of our heads,
above the earth. From that distance,
we saw our two locked bodies,
silent and still, as if the ghosts
of what gave them motion were leaving
this world. We pushed past
life and atmosphere, past
death, even, we entered
the ozone layer, and I let my wings
drop. But the seed of memory
wanted your body back,
the hardness of your supple cock
moving in me, ¾ waltz time, until
the sperm dripped from my mouth,

like the light of heaven
pouring from our mouths,
I wanted to go back.
I fell into my body, afraid
to open my eyes in case you were
a filament stuck like a metal
chromosome to my imagination,
but you were there, your wings
folded around my wings, your hand
touched the earth of my back,
then the thick syrup came
from both of us, other-worldly, I looked
straight into the spectral radiant
light pouring down through the hole
in the roof, you cried out my name,
and we took our rightful place on this earth.

PART FOUR

SACRAMENTS

1

Along lower Broadway where we walk
together for the first time, stars
of Bethlehem dangle from metal girders.
I feel your hand take my elbow, pull me
toward you as you try to tell me
something—but the sirens pulsing
and the woman screaming at the drunk
splitting his head against the railing
and the punks trying to sell me dope
are drowning out your words.
A woman pours water from a tin can
and knots the tubing at her arm, a beggar
crushes his dog's jaw with a skillet,
a man in a turban smashes a car window.
Beneath falling ice a choir sings *to save us all*
from Satan's power when we were gone astray,
and your hand slips inside my coat. I smell the gin
of your breath, the salt of your body
indistinguishable from my desire.
I move closer to you, the choir drones its melody,
the crowd jostles my body
while you kiss me beneath the blare
of horns, the ecstasy of voices, your beard
chafes my lips and cheeks, I lean
against you and you tell me your name.

Out the window snow is falling over Thirteenth Street.
I watch you pour wine from the decanter
as you tell the story: last December,
the old Italian collapsed on the icy sidewalk.
When you breathed into him, his face
became deep purple. You touch
your face when you tell me this,
and I close my eyes, see you
lying on some pavement, your face
turning purple until the blood comes
from your mouth. After the wine is gone,
my thighs grip your hips,
your hands along my ribs pull me over you
as I lean down to your lips
and hear a woman wailing for her dead husband,
chanting *Hail Marys* as she washed ash and bile
from his face, the sound of rosary, the weakness of language.

3

In church, the men in black make their bodies
invisible. I am twelve, watching the candles burn,
hearing the angels sing. The priest asks
if I will abide by my promises,
and I look at the painting of the people
carrying the body of Jesus. Shadows
strike his chest where the blood runs down
his pelvis, the muscles of his abdomen.
The loose wrap of stained cloth covering his genitals
holds my attention. Hands on his elbows, ankles,
the tapered waist. What I want is to kneel before him,
to lick the blood off, to feel his beard against my face,
to eat the wafer and call out *love* to this man.

4

Body of holiness, body of light, arms in the shape of the cross,
shadow between clefts of breast flesh, breast bone, body of pink
jewels and beard fur glistening, fine black hairs across
his chest. Words sound one syllable at a time

over the vaulted ceiling, the stone pietà whose arms cradle
the dead body, as words grant absolution, fall
like water into the porcelain bowl at the foot of our bed.
Above the altar of gardenias and gold flames

the red angel circles. I taste this strange molecular buzz,
the water I wash across his skin, the dark undergrowth
and the pink head with its salt of consummation, I kiss
this temple of pure life, I say mass on his chest.

5

Yea, though I walk through the valley of the shadow
of death, I will fear radiation

seeping through the ozone, earth's immunity.
I, a man whose ordination relies on other men,

will fear the toxins rising
from the earth's interior. I will

fear the body asleep in the other room—
anoint his skin with sacred myrrh

and lick his wounds. I will fear
rain, earth, fruit, tree: bear witness

to the fear in equal portion to the beauty.
I will fear my brother's blood, for his blood

is my own. Whatever comes of us, we will say
we lived in the valley, built a home in the shadow.

6

When Christ met the lovers on the road
the sea went still and the motorcycle stalled.
The man whose body had withered to bone
saw Christ walk toward them, his white robe
sewn with roses across the chest.
The other man wiped engine grease from his hands
then looked down at Christ's feet—
he saw blood where the nails had torn the skin.
Christ looks older than in the books, he thought,
his face wrinkled, his body slumped like an old man's.

Christ said the world had changed
since he'd walked the desert, yet he liked
the new buzz cut and the sacred heart
tattooed on the sick man's shoulder.

Christ fanned his robe over the sand,
and the fevered man slept. His lover
bent to take a cloth rose
into his oily hands: the rose
came alive in his palms, flared
like fire, and his hands became clean.

7

Along the beach suburban houses burn.
I stand inside barbed wire, watching Her
prepare almond oil, toss stones
into a basket, sift them like seeds.
She plants them along the length of wire.
I taste your blood in my mouth;
She does not want me to spit you out.

When the beach is still, I taste ash
and know that shapes are bodies rising.
At the point of each barbed wire,
a holy flower bursts forth.
Transformation is what even the sea desires.

NOTES

"Phone Sex": *"Faeries de Norteamérica, Pájaros de la Habana, Jotos de Méjico, Sarasas de Cádiz, Apios de Sevilla, Cancos de Madrid, Floras de Alicante, Adelaidas de Portugal"* is from "Oda a Walt Whitman" by Federico García Lorca.

"I do not know if sex is an illusion" is from "Dialogue" by Adrienne Rich.

"After *The Vanishing*": *The Vanishing* refers to the 1988 French/Dutch film about a woman's sudden disappearance and her boyfriend's subsequent search for her.

"Sacred Anus": The lines near the end refer to section eleven of Whitman's "Song of Myself."

"'Where Youth Grows Pale, and Spectre-thin, and Dies'" takes its title from John Keats' "Ode to a Nightingale."

Masaccio, Italian painter (1401–1428).

"Sacraments": The line ending Part Four was taken from Jean Genet's novel *Our Lady of the Flowers.*

Part Four was also inspired by a photograph by the late Bill Costa.

Part Six was written after seeing Derek Jarman's film, *The Garden.*